Table of Contents

I0169413

.... 1

Introduction 4

Roasted Mushroom and Spinach Salad 5

Shallot and Mushroom Soup 7

Baked Eggs and Fresh Herbs 9

Pork Tenderloin and Milk 11

Mint and Tomato Salad 13

Fresh Potato Salad with Parsley 15

Fresh Dill and Cucumber Salad Mix 17

Pumpkin with Rice 19

Radishes and Chopped Parsley 21

Mixture of Baby Leeks and Roasted Chicken 23

Eggs with Fresh Spinach Coated in Butter 25

Minted Syrup and Strawberries 27

Chives, Sour cream and Potatoes 29

Fresh Tomatoes and Baked Anchovies 31

Ginger and Melted Blueberries 33

Green, Mint and Braised Beets 35

Feta Drizzled with Honey and Pine Nuts 37

Collard Greens in Heavy Cream 39

Roasted Pears in Maple 41

Sweet Fresh Cherries with Kale 43

Apricots in Honey 45

Fried Cabbage with Bacon 47

Spicy Sour Cherries 49

Orange and maple glazed vegetables 51

Cherries Roasted in Honey 53

Asparagus and Eggs 55

Garden Herbs and Pheasant Wrapped in Bacon 57

Shallots with Fried Veal 59

Potato Stew and Oyster 61

Roasted Potatoes and Mackerel 63

Conclusion 65

Farm to Table Recipes that You Cannot Resist

Best Farm Fresh Recipes that You Must Try

BY: Ida Smith

License Notes

This book is licensed for your personal enjoyment only. This book may not be re-sold or given away to other people. If you would like to share this book with another person, please purchase an additional copy for each recipient. If you're reading this book and did not purchase it, or it was not purchased for your use only, then please return to your favorite ebook retailer and purchase your own copy. Thank you for respecting the hard work of this author.

Introduction

Cooking is always fun, especially when you have to cook for your loved ones. However, people are trying to avoid processed food and rather have fresh food gotten from farms or gardens. However, not everyone has a farm or garden behind their homes, but farmers have made it easier; hence, you can always visit a local market to purchase fresh food. That is why we have come up with 30 unique recipes that you can prepare from fresh produce you got from the farm or local market.

Roasted Mushroom and Spinach Salad

This is a unique garden to table recipe because almost every ingredient can be gotten from your little backyard garden, and you can enjoy a bowl of fresh salad with your loved ones.

Prep time: 40 minutes

Serves: 4

Recipes

- 8 slices of thick bacon
- 4 cups of chopped mushrooms
- 1 large well diced onion
- 1/3 cup of oil
- 2 tablespoons of lime juice
- ½ tablespoon of dried oregano
- ½ tablespoon of salt

- 8 cups of spinach

Direction

Heat up your oven to about 400 degrees. Place your rack in the middle of the oven. Divide your bacon and place them into two separate baking dish. Sprinkle your onions and mushrooms on the bacon and place in the oven. Let it roast for about 20 minutes or until your bacon becomes crispy.

Meanwhile, place your lime juice, oil, salt, oregano and a little water in a bowl, microwave it for 1 minute. Place your spinach in a bowl, scatter your roasted bacon on it, and your lime juice mixture, toss properly and serve or allow cooling before serving.

Shallot and Mushroom Soup

Soups are great for a cold winter morning and picking mushrooms from your garden for a fresh soup is the best thing that can happen.

Prep time: 40 minutes

Serves: 4

Recipes

- 1 tablespoon of butter
- 1 thinly sliced shallot
- 1 tablespoon of fresh thyme, chopped
- 1 pound of mushrooms, well sliced
- 1 tablespoon of sea salt
- 1/2 teaspoon of pepper
- 2 cups of chicken broth

- 2 tablespoons of sherry
- 2 cups of heavy cream

Direction

Melt your butter in a pan. Reduce the heat, then add your thyme and shallot and let it simmer for about 5 minutes. Add your mushrooms into the pot, sprinkle your salt and pepper, cover the pot and let your mushrooms cook until they are tender.

Add in your broth and cook for another 20 minutes, turn off heat, turn the mixture into your blender and blend until it becomes puree.

Pour into your serving dish, add your sherry and cream and serve.

Baked Eggs and Fresh Herbs

Fresh herbs are usually found in a farmer's market in abundance if you don't have them in your garden or farm.

Prep time: 15 minutes
Serves: 6
Recipes

- 8 medium sized eggs
- 1/3 cup of heavy cream
- 2 tablespoons of fresh parsley leaves well chopped
- 1 tablespoon of fresh chives
- 1 teaspoon of fresh chopped dill
- 1 teaspoon of chervil, well chopped
- 2 tablespoons of butter

Direction

Heat up your oven to about 400°. Crack your eggs into a large bowl Then, add your cream and whisk together until it is well mixed. Add your herbs to mix together and set aside.

Dissolve your butter in a pan, then pour your egg mixture into it and let it simmer for 5 minutes. Transfer the pan to the oven. Then, bake for another 5 minutes.

Remove from oven, cut into 6 wedges and serve hot.

Pork Tenderloin and Milk

You don't need to get processed pork as it contains some preservatives already, rather go for the pork that comes directly from a farmer's farm and enjoy this meal.

Prep time: 2 hours 15 minutes

Serves: 5

Recipes

- 2 pounds of pork tenderloin
- 1 tablespoon of salt
- 1 teaspoon of fresh black pepper
- 2 tablespoons of lard
- 2 cups of milk
- 2 pieces of bay leaves

Direction

Place your pork in a bowl, sprinkle your salt and pepper on it and set aside. Melt your lard in a pot, place your pork in it and simmer on each side for about 5 minutes.

Add your milk and bay leaves, cover the pot and let it cook for about 2 hours until the pork is soft. Remove from pot. Then, place on a chopping board.

Allow your milk to keep boiling until it becomes creamy sauce, cut up your meat, top with your sauce and serve in your serving dish.

Mint and Tomato Salad

When you roast tomatoes, you will notice that the flavor heightens and the sweetness develops. This flavor can be gotten from your fresh tomatoes from your farm or garden.

Preparation Time: 50 minutes

Serves: 4

Recipes

- 2 pounds of fresh cherry tomatoes
- 1 medium-sized red onion, well sliced
- 2 tablespoons of oil
- 1 tablespoon of sea salt
- 1/3 cup of fresh mint leaves, well chopped

Direction

Heat up your oven to about 400°. Line your parchment paper in a baking sheet, cut your tomatoes into halves and arrange them on your baking sheet together with your onions.

Sprinkle your oil and salt on them and roast in your heated oven for about 45 minutes until the juice from your tomatoes becomes thick like a syrup.

Remove from oven, place your tomatoes and onions in a plate, sprinkle your mint leaves on them and serve.

Fresh Potato Salad with Parsley

A simple and unique fresh from garden potato and parsley salad. It is a nice meal to start your loved ones' day.

Prep time: 20 minutes
Serves: 2
Recipes

- 4 big potatoes
- 1 tablespoon of freshly chopped parsley
- 4 pieces of anchovy fillet
- 1 tablespoon of lemon juice
- 1 tablespoon of lemon zest
- 1 tablespoon of capers
- 1 cup of mayonnaise

- ½ cup of oil
- ½ tablespoon of salt
- ½ tablespoon of black pepper

Direction

In a large pot, boil your potatoes until they are tender. Mix your oil, parsley, lemon zest, anchovies, lemon juice, and capers together in a bowl and set aside.

When your potatoes are tender, drain and let them cool a little, peel off the back and slice them round. Build your potatoes into layers on a big platter. Coat each layer with mayonnaise and place part of your parsley mixture on it. Season it with your salt and pepper to taste and serve.

Fresh Dill and Cucumber Salad Mix

There are various kinds of cucumbers gotten from the farm; hence, you can decide to go for any cucumber that you like. Getting them fresh from the farm makes this salad even more nutritious.

Prep time: 15 minutes

Serves: 4

Recipes

- 3 big cucumbers
- 1 small sized shallot, well minced
- 2 tablespoons of fresh dill, well chopped
- 1/2 cup of kefir milk
- 1/2 tablespoon of honey

- 1 tablespoon of apple vinegar
- 1/3 teaspoon of sea salt
- 1/2 teaspoon of white pepper, ground

Direction

Peel off the skin of your cucumbers and cut them into two. Remove the seeds, slice them and put in a bowl. Add your shallot and dill into the bowl and mix carefully. In a separate bowl, mix your kefir, honey, salt, vinegar and pepper and mix properly

When well coated, pour the mixture into your cucumber mixture and toss gently until well mixed and serve.

Pumpkin with Rice

Pumpkins are a lovely veggie and something you can easily get fresh from your garden; they are meaty, and preparing them with rice can make a good lunch or dinner.

Prep time: 50 minutes

Serves: 6

Recipes

- 2 tablespoons of oil
- 1 medium sized onion, well diced
- 3 cups of rice
- 1 medium sized pumpkin head, peeled and chopped
- 3 tablespoons of white wine
- 4 cups of chicken broth

- 1 sprig of rosemary, fresh
- 5 cups of fresh mushroom
- 2 tablespoons of butter
- 1/3 cup of parmesan cheese
- ½ teaspoon of salt
- ½ teaspoon of fresh ground pepper

Direction

Heat your oil in a pan and sauté your onions in the hot oil for 5 minutes. Add your pumpkin and let it cook for about 10 minutes until it is soft and continue stirring. Add your rice stir properly until it is well coated, then add your white wine.

Add part of your chicken broth into the mixture and let it boil. Add your mushrooms and rosemary to the mixture and let it simmer while you keep stirring. Let it cook until all the liquid is almost absorbed, rice tender and creamy like porridge.

Add your butter and some parmesan cheese mix properly, remove from heat. Season with your salt and pepper to taste and serve topping it with your remaining parmesan.

Radishes and Chopped Parsley

Radishes can also be gotten from your farm especially when it is the season, and preparing this recipe makes your meal nutritious and colorful.

Prep time: 15 minutes

Serves: 3

Recipes

- 14 pieces of radishes
- 2 teaspoons of butter
- 1/2 cup of well chopped fresh parsley
- 1/2 teaspoon of salt

Direction

Dice your radishes and put them in a bowl and set aside. Melt your butter in a pan, then when it foams, put your radishes into it and stir often for about 10 minutes.

Remove from pan, sprinkle your parsley and salt on it and serve while warm.

Mixture of Baby Leeks and Roasted Chicken

Leeks are a powerful and very nutritious vegetable that contains lots of nutrients making a healthy meal with it is surely amazing.

Prep time: 30 minutes

Serves: 5

Recipes

- 5 pieces of baby leeks
- 1 full chicken
- 1/2 teaspoon of salt
- 1/2 teaspoon of pepper
- 2 cups of white wine
- 1/3 cup of sherry vinegar
- 3 tablespoon of Dijon mustard
- 2 tablespoons of thyme leaves, fresh and chopped

Direction

Preheat your oven to about 400°. Chop your leeks roughly and set aside. Trim your leeks and cut them halfway and set aside. Season your chicken with salt and pepper; stuff it with the top and roots gotten from your leek.

Dry up your chicken, tie with a cooking twine, place in your baking sheet and bake until it becomes brown. Remove from oven. Then, transfer the chicken to a serving bowl and set aside.

Place your vinegar, wine and mustard in a pan, boil and remove. Garnish it with your thyme and leek and cook for another 5 minutes. Remove from heat. Serve alongside with your chicken.

Eggs with Fresh Spinach Coated in Butter

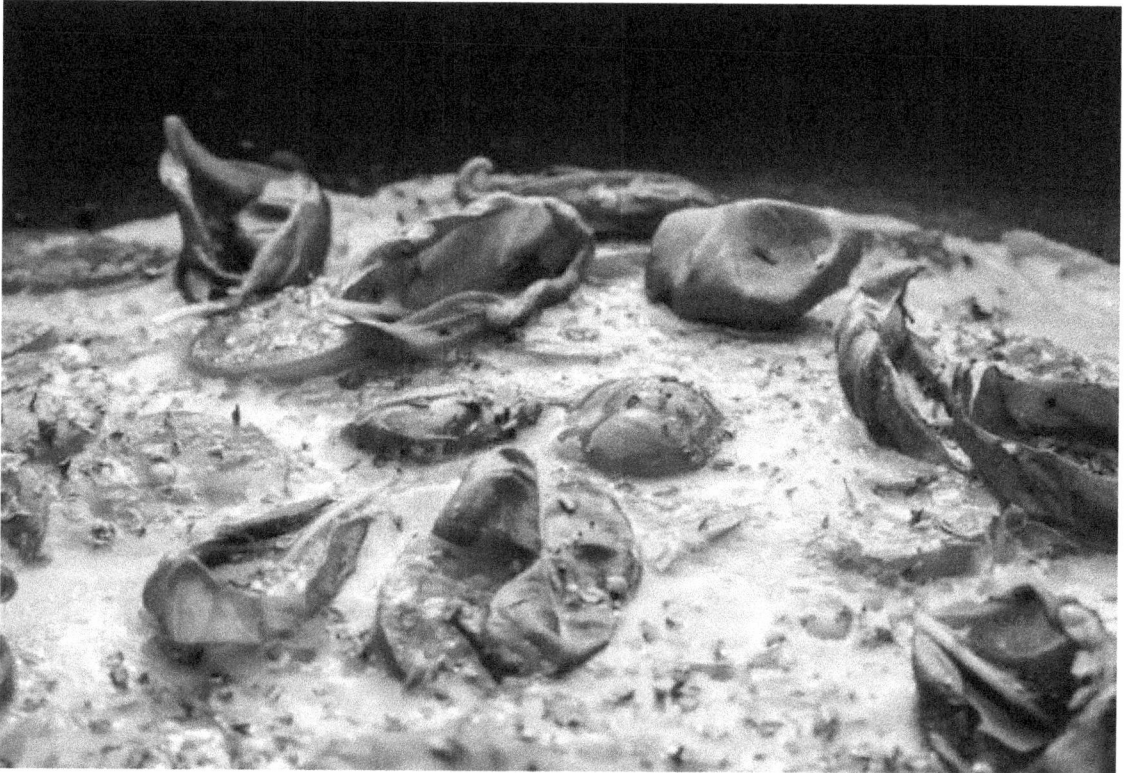

Fresh handpicked spinach from your farm or garden is very nutritious and a better dinner to serve your family.

Prep time: 30 minutes

Serves: 4

Recipes

- 2 big bunches of fresh spinach
- 1 tablespoon of butter
- Salt and pepper to taste
- 2 medium sized eggs, boiled, peeled, and well minced

Direction

Trim your spinach and remove any strong veins or stems. Chop your spinach and place it in a heavy pot, place on your stove and let it cook slowly for about 20 minutes or until it is soft.

Drain the water, remove the spinach and press down to remove excess water. Return your pot to fire, add your butter into the pot and melt it over low heat.

Add your spinach into the melted butter, add your salt, pepper and egg, coat carefully, remove from heat and serve warm.

Minted Syrup and Strawberries

Strawberries gotten from your farm are very amazing, and this combination of strawberry and mint is great.

Prep time: 30 minutes
Serves: 5
Recipes

- 1 cup of water
- 1 cup of honey
- 2 pounds of strawberries
- 1 bunch of fresh mint

Direction

In a pan, boil the water. Pour in your honey and mix until it dissolves well. Let it boil for at least 5 minutes. Then, remove pan from heat and let it cool.

Meanwhile, hull your strawberries, cut them into two and place in a bowl, pluck out the leaves from the mint stem, shred the leaves, and sprinkle on the strawberries.

Pour your homey mixture over the mint and cover, allow marinating overnight and serve.

Chives, Sour cream and Potatoes

During the late springtime, you will see the bloom of chives, and combining them with fresh potatoes gotten from your farm will make a healthy meal.

Prep time: 20 minutes

Serves: 5

Recipes

- 2 pounds of potatoes
- 1/2 cup of sour cream
- 1 bunch of chives, blossoming
- 1/2 tablespoon of sea salt
- 1/2 teaspoon of fresh ground black pepper
- 5 cups of water

Direction

Boil your water in a deep pot, add your peeled and chopped potatoes in the water and let them boil until they become tender.

Drain the water and let them cool. Place the potatoes in a bowl, add your cream, chives and chive blossom, stir properly and season with your salt and pepper and serve.

Fresh Tomatoes and Baked Anchovies

Anchovies are a very tasty and healthy dish, and preparing it with fresh veggies from your garden makes the dish even more healthy.

Prep time: 50 minutes

Serves: 4

Recipes

- 1/3 cup of oil
- 1 small sized yellow onion, diced
- 2 cloves of well chopped garlic
- 1 bulb of fennel, well trimmed and sliced
- 8 pieces of tomatoes, peeled and sliced
- 1/3 cup of white wine
- 2 pieces of bay leaves

- 2 pounds of anchovies, cleaned
- 1 teaspoon of salt
- 3 tablespoons of basil, chopped

Direction

Heat up your oven to about 360°. Heat up your oil in a pan, add your onion and garlic and let simmer for about 5 minutes, add your fennel and stir for another 2 minutes.

Add your tomatoes, white wine and bay leaves and cook for about 2 minutes until your tomatoes are tender. Spread your anchovies in a casserole dish, sprinkle your salt in them, and pour your sauce over them.

Sprinkle with basil and bake for about 40 minutes, when it is properly cooked, remove from oven and serve hot.

Ginger and Melted Blueberries

Looking for a fresh and non-processed dessert, try this combination of fresh blueberry and orange, and you will love it.

Prep time: 10 minutes

Serves: 6

Recipes

- 1 teaspoon of butter
- 1 teaspoon of fresh ginger, grated
- 3 cups of blueberries
- 1 tablespoon of honey
- 1 tablespoon of orange zest
- 1 tablespoon of orange juice

Direction

Melt your butter in a pan. Then, add your ginger and sauté for about 2 minutes. Add your blueberries, orange juice, zest, and honey. Cook until the berries are soft. Remove from heat and serve.

Green, Mint and Braised Beets

There's no better way to serve your beets than with greens. You can put this dish together in a few minutes, and it becomes a healthy meal from your farm to your table.

Prep time: 20 minutes

Serves: 6

Recipes

- 2 pounds of fresh baby beets with the greens
- 3 tablespoons of butter
- 2 cups of chicken broth
- 2 tablespoons of mint, well chopped
- 1/3 cup of apple vinegar

Direction

Remove the greens from the beets and trim the stems off. Chop the greens and set aside. Place the greens in a bowl, peel your beets and chop them and set aside.

Melt your butter in a large pan, add your beets in the pan and simmer for 4 minutes. Add your chicken broth in the pan and boil until your beets are tender.

Add your greens and mint and simmer for another 5 minutes. Remove from heat, sprinkle your vinegar on it and serve.

Feta Drizzled with Honey and Pine Nuts

Feta cheese is a bit salty, but combining it with honey and some nice and fresh from garden veggies makes a perfect light dessert.

Prep time: 25 minutes

Serves: 4

Recipes

- 1/3 cup of pine nuts
- 1 ounce of feta cheese
- 2 tablespoons of oil
- 2 tablespoons of honey
- 1 tablespoon of chopped mint
- 1 teaspoon of orange zest

Direction

Preheat your oven to about 300°. Arrange your parchment paper in a baking sheet and spread your pine nuts on it. Toast your pine nuts for about 7 minutes until they become slightly brown.

Remove pine nuts from oven and set aside. Brush your cheese with oil, place it in a baking pan and bake for about 10 minutes and remove from oven.

Place it in a broiler, sprinkle your honey on it and broil for few minutes. Dish to a serving bowl, top with your mint and zest and serve.

Collard Greens in Heavy Cream

Collard greens are often found all year round, but you get the best of collard greens during the winter period. Mixing heavy cream with your collard greens makes them more delicious.

Prep time: 15 minutes

Serves: 4

Recipes

- 1/2 cup of unsalted butter
- 1 big yellow onion, well diced
- 2 bunches of fresh collard greens, stems removed and well chopped
- 1 cup of heavy cream

- 1/2 teaspoon of grated nutmeg

Direction

Dissolve your butter in a pan over high heat, then add in your onions and sauté for about 8 minutes while stirring. Add your collards into the pan and cook for about 2 minutes.

Reduce the heat and pour your heavy cream into the pan, let it simmer for about 5 minutes, coat properly and remove mixture from pan.

Serve in your serving dish, sprinkle your nutmeg on it and serve.

Roasted Pears in Maple

You don't get only veggies from your farm or garden, but pears can also be freshly gotten from your garden or farm and used to make a lovely dessert.

Prep time: 60 minutes

Serves: 4

Recipes

- 1 tablespoon of butter
- 2 tablespoons of maple syrup
- 1/2 teaspoon of fresh nutmeg, grated
- 1/2 teaspoon of cinnamon, ground
- 1/3 teaspoon of salt
- 4 big pears, peeled, cored, and halved

Direction

Preheat your oven to about 360°. Melt your butter in a pan. Then, add your syrup, cinnamon, nutmeg and salt in it and stir. Remove from heat and place your pears into the syrup, and further scoop some syrup on your pears and roast in oven.

Roast for about 45 minutes and remove. Serve hot.

Sweet Fresh Cherries with Kale

Cherries that come directly from your garden are very fresh and taste great; preparing a meal with your fresh cherries and kale can be a better family fun time meal.

Prep time: 40 minutes

Serves: 6

Recipes

- 1/3 cup of bacon fat
- 1 small sized red onion, well diced
- 1 big apple, peeled and well diced
- 2 cups of chopped Lacinato kale leaves
- 1 cup of fresh sweet cherries
- 2 tablespoons of cider
- 1 teaspoon of apple vinegar

Direction

Dissolve your bacon fat in a pan, add your onions into the fat and simmer for about 3 minutes. Add your apple and let it simmer until it becomes tender.

Add your kale into the pan. Fry until it becomes a little soft, toss in your cherries and cider and cook until the liquid is almost dried.

Add in your vinegar, coat properly and serve.

Apricots in Honey

Take advantage of the apricot season and enjoy lots of fresh apricots directly from your farm or garden to your kitchen.

Prep time: 20 minutes
Serves: 6
Recipes

- 2 cups of white wine, sweet
- 1/3 cup of honey
- 1 vanilla bean, cut into two
- 2 pods of cardamom, ground
- 12 pieces of apricots, pitted and halved
- 2 tablespoons of mint, fresh
- 1/2 cup of whipped cream.

Direction

Mix your honey and white wine together in a pan, add your vanilla bean and cardamom and allow it to boil slowly until the honey completely dissolves.

Add your apricots and cover the pot until they are tender. Remove the apricots and transfer to a serving dish.

Allow liquid to boil, then drain out the syrup. Discard the cardamom and vanilla. Pour your syrup on the apricots, sprinkle your mint on them and serve with your whipped cream.

Fried Cabbage with Bacon

Not everyone plants cabbage, but if you get to your local markets, you will find fresh from the farm cabbages that you can use to prepare this nutritious meal.

Prep time: 25 minutes

Serves: 5

Recipes

- 1 head of savoy cabbage
- 1 tablespoon of butter
- 4 ounces of bacon, well chopped
- 2 medium sized sliced shallots

Direction

Cut your cabbage, remove the core, slice the cabbage and set aside. Melt your butter in a large pan, then add your bacon and fry until it becomes crispy. Remove from heat and set aside.

Add your shallots into the pan and simmer until they become brown. Remove the shallots and place in the bacon bowl. Toss your cabbage into the pan, fry for 10 minutes until your cabbage becomes wilted while stirring often.

Toss your shallots and bacon into the cabbage, combine properly and serve while hot.

Spicy Sour Cherries

Fresh sour cherries from your garden arrive only for a short season, but you can enjoy them while they last.

Prep time: 30 minutes

Serves: 4

Recipes

- 1/3 cup of sour cherry juice
- 1/2 cup of cans sugar, refined
- 2 pounds of fresh sour cherries, pitted and stemmed
- 1 tablespoon of ground cinnamon
- 1 teaspoon of vanilla extract
- 1/2 teaspoon of all spice, ground
- 1/2 teaspoon of cloves, ground

- 1 tablespoon of kirsch
- 1/2 cup of whipped cream

Direction

Boil your cherry juice over medium heat, add your sugar in it and stir until the sugar melts. Add your cherries into the pot, add your cinnamon, vanilla extract, cloves and all spice into the pot stir then pour your kirsch.

Cook until your cherries are soft, remove from heat, serve in your serving bowls and top with your whipped cream and serve.

Orange and maple glazed vegetables

Vegetables gotten directly from your garden are obviously fresher and healthier. Walk into your garden, pluck some carrots and paranoid veggies and prepare this sumptuous meal.

Prep time: 15 minutes

Serves: 4

Recipes

- 2 tablespoons of butter
- 3 fresh carrots, well sliced
- 1 peeled and diced parsnip
- 1/3 cup of maple syrup
- 1/2 cup of orange juice
- 2 tablespoons of freshly chopped thyme
- 1 teaspoon of salt

Direction

Melt your butter in a pan, add your carrot and parsnip into the pan and simmer for about 10 minutes while stirring occasionally. Toss your maple syrup into your veggies, add your orange juice and cook until the liquid dry off.

Remove from heat and sprinkle your thyme over the mixture, add salt, stir properly and serve.

Cherries Roasted in Honey

Cherries can be gotten from your garden, and they taste greater when they taste freshly picked, and roasting with honey makes them even better.

Prep time: 20 minutes

Serves: 5

Recipes

- 2 pounds of cherries
- 1 tablespoon of cane sugar
- 1/2 teaspoon of salt
- 1 tablespoon of kirsch
- 3 cups of heavy cream
- 1 tablespoon of vanilla extract
- 12 finely chopped honey meringues

Direction

Preheat your oven to about 400°. Remove the pits from your cherries and place them in a bowl. Add your sugar, Kirsch and salt into the bowl. Coat properly and transfer the mixture into a baking dish and roast for about 15 minutes.

Allow the cherries to cool a little. Pour your cream into a bowl, add your vanilla and whisk properly, then add your roasted cherries, add your honey, mix well and serve.

Asparagus and Eggs

Nice breakfast for a lovely weekend. Let your family wake up to this natural and freshly meal.

Prep time: 25 minutes

Serves: 6

Recipes

- 10 ounces of chopped gravlax with maple
- 6 pieces of trimmed and chopped asparagus
- 6 medium sized eggs
- 1 shallot, chopped
- 1/2 cup of heavy cream

- 1 teaspoon of fresh ground pepper

Direction

Heat up your oven to about 400°. Grease your ramekins with butter and place them on your baking sheets. Share your gravlax and asparagus equally among the ramekins.

Crack your eggs and drop them each into your ramekin. Sprinkle your shallot in the eggs, add your cream and pepper, put in your oven and bake for about 15 minutes.

Remove from oven and serve immediately.

Garden Herbs and Pheasant Wrapped in Bacon

Pheasant is a kind of bird, smaller than chicken, and its meat tastes great. Wrap it with your bacon and serve with your fresh garden herbs.

Prep time: 1 hour 30 minutes

Serves: 4

Recipes

- 3 pounds of pheasant
- 1 small yellow onion, sliced
- 2 tablespoons of fresh parsley leaf, chopped
- 2 tablespoons of fresh basil, chopped
- 1 teaspoon of thyme leaves
- 8 ounces of bacon
- 1/2 cup of white wine

Direction

Preheat your oven to about 400°. Stuff your pheasant with your onion, tie the legs together and sprinkle your herbs on it. Lay your bacon on top of your pheasant in a baking dish, pour your white wine on it and roast in your oven for about 20 minutes.

Reduce the heat and continue roasting for another 40 minutes, remove from oven, allow It to cool off a serve.

Shallots with Fried Veal

Veal is found from calves, and getting natural veal should come from calves that have been raised in the pasture; it tastes better than industrialized or processed veal.

Prep time: 20 minutes

Serves: 4

Recipes

- 1/2 cup of wheat flour
- 2 teaspoons of sea salt
- 1/2 teaspoon of ground black pepper
- 4 ounces of veal
- 2 tablespoons of fat from bacon
- 2 sprigs of rosemary, chopped
- 3 well sliced shallots

Direction

Put your flour, pepper and salt in a bowl and toss your veal into the flour mixture. Let it coat properly, then set aside.

Melt your fat in a heated pan, toss your rosemary into it and simmer for 2 minutes. Then remove and discard it. Add your shallots and simmer for about 8 minutes until they become brown.

Remove and set aside, then add your coated veal into the pan and fry for about 5 minutes, turning both sides. Top it with your shallots. Serve your veal in a serving dish.

Potato Stew and Oyster

Making stew for a cold winter morning with your fresh potatoes and delicious oysters to go with is a delicious and healthy meal for your family.

Prep time: 40 minutes

Serves: 4

Recipes

- 1 tablespoon of butter
- 1/2 leek, the white and green parts, finely sliced
- 1 big peeled and chopped potato
- 2 cups of oysters
- 2 cups of milk
- 1 bay leaf
- 1/3 teaspoon of cayenne pepper
- 1 cup of heavy cream

- 1 teaspoon of salt

Direction

Melt your butter in a pan and when it foams, add your leek and simmer for about 3 minutes until it becomes tender. Add your potato, oyster liquor, bay leaf and milk, cover your pot and let it cook for 30 minutes.

Add your cayenne pepper and oysters and cook until your oysters begin to curl, then add your heavy cream, season with salt and serve.

Roasted Potatoes and Mackerel

Fresh fish from the sea with your fresh potatoes gotten direct from your farm or garden can serve a nice dinner for your family.

Prep time: 1 hour 20 minutes

Serves: 5

Recipes

- 2 pounds of potatoes
- 6 cloves of well minced garlic
- 3 tablespoons of oil
- 1 tablespoon of salt
- 4 pounds of mackerel
- 1 medium sized lemon, sliced
- 4 sprigs of rosemary

- 4 sprigs of thyme

Direction

First, preheat your oven to about 360°. Slice your potatoes. Then, place them in a bowl and add your garlic. Add your oil and salt, mix properly to coat. Spread your potatoes in a baking dish and roast for 30 minutes.

While your potatoes are roasting, clean your mackerel rinse properly and dry with a paper towel. Stuff each mackerel with lemon, rosemary and thyme. Remove your potatoes from oven and set your mackerel on the potatoes.

Lastly, return the baking dish back to the oven and bake for another 30 minutes. Remove from oven and serve hot.

Conclusion

Fresh veggies from a farm are very healthy and nutritious. Hence, if you've been thinking of how you can use your veggies from your little garden or farm, this cookbook has provided the 30 unique recipes you can trust.

Don't miss out!

Visit the website below and you can sign up to receive emails whenever Ida Smith publishes a new book. There's no charge and no obligation.

https://books2read.com/r/B-A-LRXL-SPVKB

BOOKS 2 READ

Connecting independent readers to independent writers.

www.ingramcontent.com/pod-product-compliance
Lightning Source LLC
Chambersburg PA
CBHW081300040426
42452CB00014B/2592

* 9 7 8 1 3 9 3 6 2 2 6 5 9 *